AND HE HAD NO SONS

Written by
Thomas Ray, III

Order this book online at www.trafford.com or email orders@trafford.com
Most Trafford titles are also available at major online book retailers.

The design drawing is the original work of the author.

Printed in Victoria, BC, Canada.

ISBN: 978-1-4269-2672-3 (sc)
ISBN: 978-1-4269-2673-0 (dj)

Library of Congress Control Number: 2010901386

*Our mission is to efficiently provide the world's finest, most
comprehensive book publishing service, enabling every author to
experience success. To find out how to publish your book, your way,
and have it available worldwide, visit us online at www.trafford.com*

Trafford rev. 2/25/2010

Trafford
PUBLISHING®
www.trafford.com

North America & international
toll-free: 1 888 232 4444 (USA & Canada)
phone: 250 383 6864 ♦ fax: 812 355 4082

Dedication

This literary work is dedicated to my one and only love, Teneka Lecreia Ray. It is through my life with you, that I have come to know what it is to behold a woman with "a voice". Thank you so much for your encouragement and enduring dedication therefore I dedicate this work to you!

Acknowledgements

There are so many people to whom I desire to express my gratitude. Some were active participants in the compilation of this work, while others have not been but provided observable behaviors and encouragement that helped me compile this work. However, acknowledgement must begin with my spiritual advisors and biblical instructors in the persons of Dr. Rita L. Twiggs and Sandra Jackson, Esq. Additionally, the Discussion Board who's input was truly invaluable: Shane E. Hurley, Telethia Hurley, Michael Hurley, Alexs Donnell Harrell, Terri Bryant Harrell, Andrea Graham, Alicia B. Young, Christie Thompson, Jennifer Peete and my one and only Teneka L. Ray. Lastly, the couple that speak life to my spirit continually, Pastor Larry L. Dyer and his lovely wife Lady Natalie N. Dyer. May God bless and enrich each of your lives more than you have mine.

Contents

Numbers 26:29-34 KJV

v.29 "Of the sons of Manasseh: of Machir, the family of the Machirites: and Machir begat Gilead: of Gilead come the family of the Gileadites.

v.30 These are the sons of Gilead: of Jeezer, the family of the Jeezerites: of Helek, the family of the Helekites:

v.31 And of Asriel, the family of the Asrielites: and of Shechem, the family of the Shechemites:

v.32 And of Shemida, the family of the Shemidaites: and of Hepher, the family of the Hepherites.

v.33 And Zelophehad the son of Hepher had no sons, but daughters: and the names of the daughters of Zelophehad were Mahlah, and Noah, Hoglah, Milcah, and Tirzah.

v.34 These are the families of Manasseh, and those that were numbered of them, fifty and two thousand and seven hundred."

Preface

So often in life people find themselves at a disadvantage. The reasons for such can approach infinity, but there are those disadvantages which seem to arise from the absence or neglect of another. In such cases, discouragement can overcome an individual and change one's posture. One can migrate from a posture of strength and confidence to weakness and disillusionment.

Furthermore, one's body language and speech can echo the emotions bound on the inside. Some become quiet, even mute. Others begin to spew and hurl words of discouragement and speak as one who is down trodden and defeated. Yet and still, others become angry and their vocabulary and language resound infuriation. Why?

This is a difficult question to approach but many have found themselves victimized by systems and processes that are unable to consider all possible circumstances. At times, people fall prey to the penalties of law, yet have committed no crime. Such would be a case of mistaken identity. In these situations, people become especially emotional because they are penalized having committed no crime.

What then shall be said of penalties without crime? What can be said for wages of sin where no sin is found? Scripture denotes so much, especially in the Law of Moses pertaining to sin and the penalties of such but nothing was noted about falling prey to penalty when there was no sin initially. How does this occur? How can it be stopped? How do you receive blessing when a curse is bound for you? Read on and discover how to escape the penalty of law when no crime has been committed.

Prologue

Moses, the great man of God is now engaging in the second numbering of Israel. In all actuality, Moses is taking the second census. The first generation of Israeli's delivered from Egypt forfeited their inheritance with disobedience and rebellion. Now, their children, who they alleged would be as prey to the inhabitants of Canaan were in position to inherit the promised land of God as if they were the firstborn.

This task, no doubt is quite an intense one and Moses is careful to conduct such with caution. The numbering of Israel in this census was for war and inheritance. The needs of Israel as a nation were to be met through warfare. Once in the promised land, it was imperative that each tribe receive land sufficient for their number.

As it relates to war, the census was not to capture everyone in the nation. God did not want Israel to number themselves as other nations did, thereby building their confidence upon the number of people in the nation. Therefore, God numbered only men aged 20 and older. Women, children, and recently married men were exempt from war.

As it relates to inheritance, the census was taken by tribes first. Once a tribe was gathered, then the heads of each family brought forth their family for numbering. When that family was presented, the heads of each of those individual families presented themselves. They were then numbered for inheritance.

Following this, no census should have ever been taken. Of special mention, should be the reality that in the census only the heads of the households are named. Everyone else is counted but unnamed. Throughout the first census you find the aforementioned to be true. However, in the second census an abrupt change is made. At the numbering of the tribe of Manasseh, a man by the name of Hepher is mentioned. Nothing is mentioned about Hepher himself but his son Zelophehad. It is found that Zelophehad had no sons but daughters and they are named. Peculiar instance seeing that no other family head mentioned had any of his family members named, male or female.

How peculiar is this abrupt change in the reasonable flow of events? As callous as it may seem, why is Hepher most known for his son Zelophehad? Normally in scripture it is the father's name which carries weight for the son. However, in this instance Hepher, the father of Zelophehad is known for his son, who has been unable to bring forth any sons himself.

Not much is said about Zelophehad other than the fact that he had no sons but five daughters. The entire mention is illogical in the reasonable progression of events in this text. Speculation lends that such a reality must be the will of God.

But really, why are these women noted in the census? Who are these women and for what purpose are they mentioned? What mystery does God seek to unveil through these five women who have never been seen prior to their mention?

SECTION I:
THE VOICE OF A WOMAN

One of the most unassuming and powerful persons on the face of God's earth is a woman with "a voice". The usage of the word "voice" in this context does not refer to one having a functioning voice box because such does not permit the assumption that "a voice" is present. It is not the physicality of the production of sound from within the human body that is neither noteworthy nor relevant in this case.

To suggest "a voice" predicates that a woman has come into contact with two critical elements, which yield "a voice". The first critical element would be the revelation of "God's Righteous Cause". With such revelation, the second of the two critical elements manifests, which is the call or "purpose" of God. It's manifestation in the life of a woman becomes a compass whereby "God's Righteous Cause" is made known to mankind, in order that His Holy will be done.

Having discovered her purpose in the shadow of the light of God's Righteous Cause, a woman can then allow herself to become infatuated with it. It is as a consuming fire that eradicates any ancillary agendas and fixes her focus on God, His Cause, and her purpose in making His will known. Armed and equipped, she can now push forward into society for her voice is birthed and she will become iconic in her arena and era.

The Birth of a Woman's Voice

*"So God created man in his own image,
in the image of God created he him; male and
female created he them." (Genesis 1:27 KJV)*

To those who confess Jesus Christ as Lord, the annals of Jewish Antiquity hold for us the most important history. It holds the beginning of all things and all people. Specifically, the book of Genesis reveals the beginning of God's will in the earth. So it is here, the "voice" is first noted.

Indeed, at the outset of Genesis 1:27, the woman has yet to manifest for she is still incubating within the man. However, she is an inheritor of everything God has made for man. She will operate coequally with the man to ensure the will of God is done. Once the place of habitation is prepared and the will of God disclosed, the man is put to sleep while the "help meet or helper" is extracted from within him. She stands beside him in everything pertaining to the will of God for

3

their existence, that she might help him in the immense work before him. The beauty of marriage is revealed where two are actually one in the sight of God and it takes the two to bring the one command to pass.

By design, the woman comes to being as a co-executor of God's will. She is made to ensure the will of God is done to its completeness; nothing is to be left out or unattended. God is quite a detailed being and by nature women are as well. The miniscule detail will more than likely be ignored by man but attracts the stark attention of the woman. Therefore, the two, who are actually one, suit the will of God for the garden well. According to scripture, "The Lord God took the man and put him in the Garden of Eden to work it and take care of it" (Genesis 2:15 NIV). Certainly, man is equipped to work the garden, but its care is solely the focus of the woman.

It is to this end that her voice becomes apparent. Her presence alone suggests that man was not complete and God's will, would not be either. Therefore, her voice, her ability to articulate thoughts, ideas, and notions becomes tantamount to the fulfillment of man's purpose and task in the earth which is to "be fruitful and multiply, and replenish the earth, and subdue it: and have dominion over the fish of the sea, and over the fowl of the air, and over every living thing that moveth upon the earth." (Gen. 1:28 KJV) These things can only be effectuated with the help of the woman and the all too obvious employment of her voice. She is created to have a voice!

Consider This.....

As it pertains to this work, to speak shall hold the definition of one utilizing his/ her mouth in conjunction with the necessary organs and systems within the body to articulate thoughts, ideas, sounds, etc... To speak is something humans have the capacity to perform. Even babies speak or make sounds that suggest a language is being spoken. Caretakers attempt to do all they can to decipher what the baby is saying. However, to have a voice suggests that one has purposeful communication. Here, all of the faculties utilized to speak are focused in a specific area and governed by holy purpose fueled by the motivation of God.

The Death of a Woman's Voice

*"But of the tree of the knowledge of good
and evil, thou shalt not eat of it: for in
the day that thou eatest thereof thou
shalt surely die." (Genesis 2:17 KJV)*

Although the length of time is unknown to many, the death
of the woman's voice comes with such dismay. It is a most
certain tragedy. The loss of her voice creates a vacuum in the
earth. An imbalance replaced the homeostatic environment
created by God. Why? What happened?

The loss or death of the woman's voice is due to disobedience and pride. The woman, who is named Eve in her fallen
estate, has fallen from co-executor of God's will to the position of one being ruled. This is the result of an inappropriate
conversation with the adversary of God. The conversation
between she and Satan leaves much to be desired for Adam,
who was with her and offered no comment, rebuttal, or

protection for her. However, her desire to hear more about the Tree of Knowledge of Good and Evil reveals her yearning for additional knowledge about the forbidden.

Unsatisfied with the information disseminated by the Creator, the woman seeks what might appear to be further enlightenment about the "Tree". Her decision to inquire further at the hand of an enemy results in her being stripped of her voice and position. She lost all because of a perversion from Satan that she held as truth. So it is, she goes from a position of equality, "a help meet or helper", to a servant or one being ruled. (Gen. 3:16)

Dear Daughter,

You must be gasping for breath at this moment. Ruled! Ahhh! Take a deep breath and exhale. Hear this truth: these things were of no surprise to God. There is an important application for your life however. Total subjection to another will render you mute. This is the converse of the purpose of mankind as outlined in Genesis 1:28. God always finishes what he begins and He is not finished with you. Remember, if you have or shall ever lose something given to you by God, such as the prized possession of your "voice" just recall Christ's answer to Nicodemus "ye must be born again". (John 3:7 KJV)

The Rebirth of a Woman's Voice

"And in that day thou shalt say, O Lord, I will praise thee: though thou wast angry with me, thine anger is turned away, and thou comfortedst me." (Isaiah 12:1 KJV)

From Eve to Sarah, it is evident that the estate of the woman has fallen, as did that of the man. Howbeit, the man became a ruler over the woman. In other words, she became mute or a subject of the man. This became the fate of all women, regardless of their lineage. As time progressed, even the names of women were forgotten or ignored. Finally, it gets to the point where their existence is unnoted. It is as if her existence is a vapor, only recognized through contextual clues, for man has no ability to bear children so one must assume that he had a wife. This is a most grievous judgment.

However, her estate did not remain forever like this. As mankind populated the earth, God was drawn to the worship of a man in the land of Ur. With him, God made a covenant, or a binding agreement where man is responsible for maintaining faithfulness and obedience and God takes on the greater responsibility of fulfillment. The man to whom God counted faith for righteousness is Abram.

It is not just given to the realization that God entered into a covenant with Abram that draws and merits attention. God had already entered and made an everlasting covenant with Noah after the flood. Therefore, one must derive that there is a greater purpose at work in this instance. With the covenant established between Abram and God, he separates from his family. By faith he moves forward into the land of promise and as he does so the true family is reborn.

Abram is not alone nor is any assumption necessary pertaining to this. It is most recognized that he has a "help meet or helper". His "help meet or helper" is also named and she is Sarai. Once again, the woman exists and even thrives. She is duly noted by a name and recognized by her husband and her God. With such recognition comes a renewal, a refreshing, and regeneration. Standing, with her husband, in the light of God she obtains what no woman prior to her had the opportunity to acquire. She has been granted the wish or prayer of every woman between her and Eve. She is the first recipient of the re-born "voice" of the woman.

Sarai is granted "a voice" after the covenant is fixed and in place. Again, just as it was with the initial man, the place is prepared and then the woman is extracted in order that she might be the "help meet or helper" in the effectuation of the will of God. Likewise, Sarai is brought forth with Abram in order to do the will of God. Interestingly enough, she was a barren woman and unable to bear Abram any children. However, her worth to Abram was far greater than child bearing alone and in defiance to the cultural norms of the day, Abram kept her as his sole wife until her death. Even when Abram mirrored Adam and neglected to speak up for his wife in Egypt, God intervened. He protected and preserved Sarai for her "voice" was far to important to the will of God to allow for any invasion on her purity.

The rebirth of the woman's voice in the life of Sarai takes yet another turn. Once the seal of the covenant is given, that of circumcision, God enlightens the world to the greater work of Abram and Sarai. God desires to be as close to them as possible and therefore provides both with a "rebirth", representative in the changing of their names. To Abram, God inserts the "ah" from his personal name Jehovah (Yahweh in Hebrew) into the midst of Abram's name renaming him Abraham, a father of many nations. To Sarai, God reveals her coequal status by placing the same "ah" from his personal name Jehovah at the end of her name. In other words, she was made to ensure the completion of the will of God in the earth and to care for the fine details. Therefore, the "i" is replaced with an "ah" and she goes from Sarai to Sarah. Jehovah completes her!

The name change is significant for Abram to become Abraham but it is paramount for Sarai to become Sarah. The curse of Eve is obliterated in the life of Sarah.

It died with the name of Sarai, for truly "I" is the source of pride, which was fuel for Eve's fall. This "I" is displaced in the life of Sarai. The "I" is destroyed and replaced with the essence and spirit of Jehov'ah". She becomes Sarah, the queen mother of the descendents of Abraham, even without a child of her own. She is one flesh with her husband and one in the spirit with God. Sarah!

Dear Daughter,

I told you! What God begins He will complete. The conversion of Sarai to Sarah and the rebirth of her voice show us the greatness of God. God truly is great and He is great in you. Culturally, Sarah was a reproach because she had no children but spiritually she was golden because she loved God. Do you get it? What society deems as important is not what God looks upon when He desires to bless you. Are you barren in any way? Do not place your focus on what is barren but rather on the will of God. When you do this, God will intervene and remove the stumbling block of "I" and replace it with "ah", making you one in the spirit with Him. You shall bear much fruit daughter, much fruit!

Three Women: A Parable

"All these things spake Jesus unto the multitude in parables; and without a parable spake he not unto them:..." (Matthew 13:34-35 KJV)

There were three women standing in the marketplace. One woman was quite outspoken and demanded the attention of all within earshot of her. She appeared confident and had definite ideas and opinions about a variety of things. She was known for "speaking her mind" and "calling it like she saw it".

Her comrade hardly spoke a word at all. She nodded her head to just about everything her outspoken friend stated. In many instances, one might forget she was ever present in the marketplace for she hardly spoke. Her boisterous friend stated she was a shy woman and not one to have many words.

Another woman in the marketplace was one of a more reserved manner. You might say, she was neither loud nor quiet. She did not peruse the marketplace much, but attended the same booths and carts

17

consistently week after week. She is quite difficult to decipher because she is so discreet in her dealings. Some of merchants she frequented have explained to other merchants in the marketplace that she has cultivated strong business relationships with them and they appreciate her business. You might say she is a reserved lady of simple, yet fine apparel. She always has a kind word to speak and unknown to many she is quite a community activist howbeit she prefers to operate behind the scenes. Occasionally, when the situation mandates such, she states her thoughts and opinions openly and all attend to her words because she has a way of pricking the heart and mind of others.

It is at these moments when the boisterous woman becomes combative. She is not a fan of the reserved woman. The shy woman simply watches the two. She listens to her boisterous friend jeer and mock the reserved woman. She listens to her boisterous friend talk about her choice in clothing, proper diction, and her "do good" attitude. She alleges that the reserved woman's motives are not as pure as they may seem.

Interestingly enough, the reserved woman never answers or addresses the boisterous woman. She simply smiles, nods, or shakes her head ever so gently. She never addresses the boisterous woman directly but often indirectly through the use of her speech or statement. The shy woman has heard the reserved woman on several occasions and has observed that she never veers from her message. She remains focused regardless of circumstances surrounding her. It is as if she is fixed, purposefully, onto the words that proceed from her mouth. Each new word she speaks is connected to the preceding word spoken. It is amazing. Her communication is sharp, direct, thought provoking, and heart touching.

Although befriended by the boisterous woman, the shy woman has always admired the reserved woman. She has even been guilty of envy. From the shy woman's perspective, the reserved woman has so much purpose and direction. All of her energy and effort is devoted to her purpose, which she understands clearly and her voice illuminates such, very well.

Now tell, which of the three women are you?

The Woman with a Voice

The woman with a voice is one of strength, focus, and purpose. She is quite a person. She may not have always maintained her current stature in life but certainly she is settled and fixed on that which is important to her.

It should be duly noted that the woman with "a voice" is committed to God. Her commitment however is far beyond religion. Her commitment is rooted in relationship. The woman with "a voice" is a staunch worshipper of God, even beyond corporate worship service. This woman maintains an intimate relationship with God and looks for His hand in all things pertaining to her life. She upholds His righteous cause and is an avid and active supporter of it. Thus, her spiritual constitution is based in God's Word and His Work, even His move in mankind.

She is a woman that has received an impartation from God. Such is granted to her that she might serve her generation. A unique and innate impact is slated to be made in her lifetime and she is one of its conduits. She is more than a woman of eloquent speech, for she may be one of limited speech. It is not the quality or cultivation of her words that make the impact but that which she carries in her spiritual bosom that is the differentiating factor.

Within her spiritual bosom, she carries the burden of the Lord. She has been strengthened in order that she might be able to bear the weight it. Literally, she is carrying the righteous cause of God for mankind that will revolutionize her community in her time. As it was with Sarah, she carries the Word of the Living God which shall bring hope, liberty and enlightenment.

Such a woman is careful to protect what the Lord has placed within her. Therefore, she refrains from simple, frivolous conversation that tends to rob one of their spirituality. With that in mind, most often she is a woman of very few friends and sufficient enough acquaintances. Her social circle is a very limited one and to that end she is satisfied. Her public appearances are mostly relegated to events which relate to those causes she holds dear. In other words, the woman with "a voice" does not attend functions for the sake of attending but those functions are somehow connected to God's righteous cause. Being discreet and modest however, often subjects her to the ridicule of others, especially women who operate by "noise".

The Woman with Noise

Elementary as it may seem, the word "noise" has a negative connotation. "Noise" is often associated with that which is uncomfortable, undesirable, and not admirable. When considering "noise" people often cringe at the mention of the word. It is likened unto unorganized sound, which is unpleasant to the ear and even retched to the soul. Loud clamorous-like cymbals clashing without regard to any organized music score is a common thought or even the sound of an angry teacher's finger nails scratching a chalk-board to gain the attention of an out of control class is another.

Another example of "noise" is commentary. Of course, commentary is often pleasant or at least civil but there is a commentary that is cluttered, senseless, and void of value. Such commentary has often been the reason for the conclusion of relationships between friends and lovers. This sort of biased, untried commentary tends to repulse others. Depending upon their station in life and their personal confidence level, this determines how they deal with such a person that utilizes this form of communication. In short, it is this type of commentary that is regarded as "noise".

Most often a woman with "noise" is called the "squeaky wheel" and people comply with her requests in order to quiet her commentary. However, unbeknownst to her is the vantage point of others. Specifically, how she is viewed and even regarded. In reality, by those who understand the true aspects of social responsibility and appropriateness, she is but a fool. (Proverbs 9:13). In her attempt to be regarded, she is disregarded. The woman with "noise" has forsaken the all too important task of education and research and merely spews her untried commentary on others. She will either draw like minded women or dominate those with "no voice". However, by those with a "voice" a woman with "noise" is dismissed.

The question then becomes, why would a woman employ "noise" opposed to a "voice"? The answer is both simple and complex. It is the root of the matter that must be explored. How does a woman evolve into an abrasive, irritating, and self absorbed being? It can only be speculated, but certainly has been debated that such a woman that speaks senselessly from a self-absorbed position has been disregarded throughout life. In an effort to be regarded or gain the attention of others, she employs "noise". Is it not true with children some attention is better than none? Therefore, making "noise" draws attention and young girls require attention for various reasons. Unless rectified early, this behavior or method matriculates throughout life and becomes known to us as the woman with "noise".

The Woman with No Voice

The woman with "no voice" is quite a phenomenon. This woman hardly ever speaks, especially in public. She is either regarded as very shy or is completely invisible, in a figurative sense. Her thoughts, conscience, ideas, and opinions are unshared and unspoken by her. She is virtually a mute person. Why would someone behave in this manner? What would cause an individual to basically withdraw from society in such a way as to forego the natural humanistic tendency to communicate with others and share thoughts and ideas?

As with the woman with "noise", this woman too has been subjected to environmental challenges that resulted in her "no voice" status. It is important to understand, it is not that she is void of conscience, thoughts, ideas, or creativity. It is not that she is mentally challenged at all. More often than not she has been subjected to an environment or system that has, through various means, withdrawn her voice from her.

In many cultures throughout the world, a woman with "a voice" is regarded as brash, unruly, or vexed and should be punished, even with death. In other cultures, where male dominance is the norm, a woman with "a voice" or "noise" is abused in an effort to quiet her. A woman with "a voice" or "noise" presents a challenge to her male counterpart and can be viewed negatively, even in Western Culture.

Be they covert or overt, systems exist to ensure that women are without "a voice" so that certain cultures are able to function easily without question. For if a focus is placed on silencing a woman, proper focus will not be placed on socio-economic issues that are far more important to the lives of everyone in that society. In short, it is a diversion by the aristocratic. If men, regardless of their socio-economic status are empowered through the silencing of their woman or women, then the need for economic gain and intellectual elevation is non-existent, for the man is in a position of power. Superficial as it may seem, it is a harsh reality.

Is this the will of God? Some may say that all do not believe in the God of Abraham, Isaac, and Jacob. This may be a fact, however the truth of the matter is "The earth is the Lord's and the fullness thereof, the world and they that dwell therein" (Psalm 24:1-2 KJV). The will of God, the creator, Jehovah is that all work together, male and female, to fulfill his will in the earth without oppression.

The aforementioned instances are more extreme. The environment, mores, and even laws support such. However, there are women throughout the world, in free societies, where their voice has been taken.

Just as extreme as it may seem to many in the United States that a woman is legally and culturally deprived of "a voice", there are many, even countless women in the United States, Europe, Australia, etc that are bereft of "a voice". How can this be? So often, women lose their "voice" in free societies through oppression. Physical, mental, and emotional abuse has robbed women of "a voice". The impending threat of abuse will cause a woman to withdraw and restrict herself from speaking with any authority or responsibility. Even in the workplace, discrimination rages and women have to be silent, or work ridiculous hours to make their male superior appear completely competent. If she speaks out pertaining to such abuse, because it is an abuse of power, she is retaliated against and life there becomes unbearable. She may even be "black balled" and unable to find comparable work. Therefore, she is silent, with "no voice". In the home, where an abusive husband rages, be it physical, mental, or emotional, women are inclined to cower and exist without "a voice" for fear of harm.

What then is the difference between societies where such is acceptable and legal, and those where it is culturally and legally unacceptable? The previous mentioned suggests there is not much difference other than the possibility of receiving reparations should one be in position to pursue legal action. In most cases, these women are left as the women who lived from Eve unto Sarai; existing but not thriving much less contributing.

What's the Conclusion of the Matter?

It can be surmised that to have "a voice" is of far greater value than to be either "noisy" or with "no voice". That much is simple. However, there is a profound truth present in this as well. That is, God's intention. Man so often has various methods and ways to ensure the promulgation of his desires and wishes through carefully designed systems. In order for true multiplication and dominion to occur in the lives of people, as was the original intent of mankind, a proper perspective is necessary. That is to say, men and women alike must come together truly as ONE. Sexism, genderism, racism, and classism must be returned to their place of origination, Hades! They must be expelled from the presence of families throughout the world in order for all to walk as true kings, queens, and priests of the Most High. Therefore, further examination is required to reveal how such a stratospheric jump can transpire. It has happened before, in ancient times and it can happen again in these present times!

Dear Daughter,

Quick question: which of these women are you? I know it is rather forward but the approach is necessary. Tell yourself the truth. It is vital. The reason this is so vital is because you must make the stratospheric jump mentioned above. It is not as difficult as it may seem or appear to be. If you have been truthful with yourself, then it is possible to change your method of operation. For instance, if you are a "noisy" woman, and you have been honest with yourself in admitting this, then you will be able to make the transition to a woman with "a voice" rather smoothly. If you are a woman with "no voice", you too can make the transition to a woman with "a voice" just as smoothly. How so? Simply, gain the proper knowledge and perspective of the "kingdom" to which you hail, assuming you are a child of God. If not, become one, for "a voice" awaits every representative of Gods' kingdom.

SECTION II:
THE LAW OF THE LAND

Kingdom of Priests

*"although the whole earth is mine, you
will be for me a kingdom of priests
and a holy nation."(Ex.19:5b KJV)*

The nation of Israel, as it was in this day, even unto today, is a
most peculiar nation. They were not to be as other nations,
which surrounded them. They were to be different by design.
Their methods and ways, their customs and mores, were not
derived from earthly understanding, representing the carnal
desires of mankind, but rather were delivered unto them from
on High.

Most often when one thinks of a kingdom spiritual
thoughts do not follow. Kingdom and all of the connotations
involved with it is a term reserved for political and military
prowess. It speaks to the power of a monarch to rule a nation
and defend it as well through the use of a most obedient mili-

tary. What is not often regarded when the word kingdom is employed is priest(s).

The priest is regarded as the spiritual aspect of mankind, the person who stimulates the moral conscience of individuals. The priest ensures the education of Godly principles to mankind. He/She also performs rituals that pertain to God and His relationship with His people. Priests provide counsel and help parishioners or citizens through difficult circumstances. They also show to whom they counsel the hand of God in the matter. However, one thing that a priest does not do is rule a nation.

However, in the most peculiar way, God regards Israel as a Kingdom of Priests. They are to be a holy nation set apart for God's use. Israel becomes the model nation for other nations who do not regard God as sovereign. The power and influence of Israel was to be noted by their relationship to God and His power flowing through them. Other nations would fear Israel, not because of their numbers or military might, but because of the God they serve and His fierce strength which He exudes on their behalf.

Within this Kingdom of Priests, the manner in which the economy operated was unique. The laws and regulations which governed the economy were in stark contrast to that of other nations. Israel, truly was set apart for God's use. Israel was to be God's shining example of life with Him as the center.

National Economic Policy

*"And the Lord appeared unto Abram,
and said, Unto thy seed will I give
this land" (Genesis 12:7a KJV)*

The economic policy of Israel was of most significant contrast to that of other nations. Their national monetary policy and trade policy (internal and external to Israel) were nothing like those of other nations. The way in which debt was created, paid, or dissolved was in stark contrast to the systems recognized by other nations. Their overall fiscal policy was based on honesty and forgiveness, which would continually promote growth and blessing. Their fiscal market operated like no other fiscal market ever known to man prior to the birth of Israel as a nation of people.

As an agriculturally focused nation, land was the basis upon which individuals obtained both sustenance and wealth It was the integral asset of Israel. The beauty of this is found in the way in which land ownership evolved. Upon entry into the promised land, at the hand of Moses and then again at the hand of Joshua, Moses' successor, land was distributed to every tribe in Israel. Within each tribe, land was distributed to clans, and within each clan land was distributed to each family. No one was left without access and ownership of the most important asset in Israel, land.

Why is land the basis of God's economy? God created the earth and commanded man to execute dominion over it. From the outset, man was to rule the earth. So it is apparent then, that land is the basis of the economy in Israel because God is once again establishing man in a prepared place in the earth. For Adam it was Eden but for the descendants of Abraham it is Canaan. Both are prepared places for God's elect creation.

Therefore, God's relocation of Israel as a nation from Egypt to Canaan was done to fulfill his promise to Abraham and to establish the heavenly example in the earth. God's throne is in heaven and man's throne is in the earth. Therefore, the operations of Israel on earth are to be replicas of God's operations in heaven. To that end, Israel is to be the shining example, a beacon of light to nations who are unaware of the darkness in which they live. Israel was to be such a light, that other nations desired their life and the source of such, which would result in their yearning for the God of Israel to be their God.

Land Rights and Laws

Of particular mention, in terms of their ways, is their perspective and governance as it pertains to land rights and ownership. Israel's real estate policies and procedures are most peculiar (in a good way). Initially, the real estate which was used to provide Israel with a homeland was purchased by God through repossession.

Many have debated the reason for God choosing Canaan as the homeland for Israel. Regardless of any stance, Canaan was promised to Abraham and God always keeps and fulfills His promises. However, in reflection, to place Israel at the center of influence, travel routes, and what some coin as the earth, is the perfect location to showcase a shining example. Therefore, if the current inhabitants do not reflect what God is looking for in that location, expulsion becomes necessary, especially in the shadow of a tall promise made to a man whom God said was righteous because of his belief in Him.

Therefore, God states to Abraham, "In the fourth genera-tion, your descendants will come back here, for the sin of the Amorites has not yet reached its full measure." (Gen. 15:16 NIV) Abraham, the man to whom the land was originally promised was informed by God Himself how the transfer of ownership would occur in terms of the land. Based upon the High Holy Law of God, the transfer of land is performed when the inhabitants of the land sin, abide in iniquity, beyond that which the land can bear. In other words, "The earth is the

Lord's and the fullness thereof, the world and they that dwell therein" (Ps. 24:1KJV) One may not regard the true and living God, consider Him as God, or acknowledge that He exists, but they are still subject to the High Holy Law of God and will reap accordingly.

SECTION III:
APPEAL TO THE
HIGHER COURT

The High Holy Law of God

"For my thoughts are not your thoughts,
neither are your ways my ways, saith
the Lord." (Isaiah 55:8 KJV)

What is this "High Holy Law of God?" In my opinion, it is the innate nature of God. It is His way of governing heaven and earth, without contradiction and free of violation. It is His thought process, His emotions, His very essence, which can not be completely captured and articulated in any language, nor comprehended by any school of thought. However it can be understood by them that love Him. The matters of the heart, when one's heart strives after God, become a bridge from that which is understood (and often misunderstood) to that which is revealed.

The High Holy Law of God moves one from operating by factual means to that which is based upon truth. Facts do not always lead to truth, as they can be strung together in any order to convey any position. By doing this, facts therefore can be ordered to possibly declare a lie. Such a misuse of facts occurred in the wilderness when Jesus was fasting and being tempted of the Devil. Satan said, "If thou be the Son of God, command that these stones be made bread." (Matt. 4:3 KJV) The fact is Jesus contained the spiritual authority and ability to turn stone to bread. However the truth is found in Christ's response, "It is written, Man shall not live by bread alone, but by every word that proceedeth out of the mouth of God." (Matt. 4:4 KJV) Here it can be found that truth always stands and declares the position of God on any matter. It had been forty days and forty nights since Christ had eaten but the approach of Satan with facts, which he would have later aligned to corrupt the Son of God are destroyed by truth. The beauty of truth is that it will stand in contrast to that which is reasonable and acceptable, enduring harsh ridicule and making one vulnerable. None the less, at the close of the matter, truth will speak and leave many confounded.

So, be assured, God has ways and methods of dealing that are not like mankind. God has a law that He Himself must honor, that often stands in contrast to what is accepted by man. He can be compelled to bless or deliver beyond the written law's ramifications should one touch His heart. Therefore, if God has made a promise to you, regardless of the law of the land's position, He will keep and fulfill it.

The Mosaic Law

Students of the bible have read and somewhat understood the basic tenants and confines of the Mosaic Law. The Mosaic Law is summarized in the ten-commandments. By abiding and adhering to the ten basic commandments of God, citizens of Israel could remain reasonably holy as it pertains to the Law of Moses. Understanding that God gave Moses the law, does not super cede the truth that God gave Abraham a promise. In other words, the Law of Moses stands subject to the promise of Abraham. How so?

Abraham had no law. Abraham walked with God and believed every word God spoke to Him. His belief positioned him to obtain an eternal covenant with God for his descendants. The descendants of promise are those who are birthed after the promised son, Isaac. Isaac is the son God gave Abraham and his wife Sarah in their very old age, being 100 and 90 respectively. Isaac is a miracle because of their age and stands in stark contrast to any other son born at that time, especially in the house of Abraham. The birth of Isaac is the initiation of covenant blessings passing from a Father to the chosen son. Isaac becomes the inheritor of the Abrahamic Covenant blessings. The beauty of this is that no law dictated any of the aforementioned. Belief in God was the key factor.

The purpose of the Law of Moses or the Mosaic Law was to provide framework for social conduct, worship, and moral conscience. The Law of Moses was given to ensure the mind and will of God was communicated to the people of God in a simple way. It was given to expose sin and provide sound judgment for such as to hinder the propagation of ill behavior. However, the Mosaic Law was not given to prevent men and women from thinking. It was not given to hinder men and women from pursuing higher thoughts and enhancing their relationship with God. Unfortunately, the mindset of many would be to rest at the point of what is written and negate pursuit of a more intensified revelation. So often, we find today, believers still living in the mindset of legality when Christ has given liberty. Many just don't realize there is a law above all law. Such was the reality in Israel, even among Moses and his comrades as the book of Numbers draws to a close.

Who Are Zelophehad's Daughters?

*"And Zelophehad the son of Hepher had
no sons, but daughters: and the names
of the daughters of Zelophehad were
Mahlah, and Noah, Hoglah, Milcah,
and Tirzah" (Numbers 27:1b KJV)*

There is a question that arises from the pages of the ancient
scriptures that is not visible but is yet contextual. Who are
these women? How is it that they arrive at the Tabernacle and
gain an audience with Moses? Based upon the consultative
work done by Jethro, the Midianite Priest, the father-in-law
of Moses, a council was created to alleviate the burden of
listening to all of the problems of the multitude of Israelites.
Jethro suggested that Moses select able men, who fear God,
relish truth, are not covetous and let them judge the smaller
matters. Only the most difficult matters were to come to

Moses. By doing this, Moses would not "wear away" as Jethro stated.

In light of this council, which Moses adhered strictly to, one can almost envision Zelophehad's daughters beginning their journey to the Tabernacle. First, it began right in their own tribe, probably with a family member who was the head of Machir's family. Stumped as we can imagine, this family head passed them on to a clan head. Stumped as we can image, they were then passed on to the tribal head. Stumped as we can image, they were then passed on to the priest's, who were unable to provide a sound answer to Zelophehad's daughters. At this point, they must go before the man who speaks with God face to face, for this matter is too great for any other. Zelophehad's daughters receive their day at the Tabernacle. They will plead their cause to the Man of God, Moses.

Dear Daughter,

I have a word of advice for you. Do not become disenfranchised when you are seemingly passed along through various men, women, committees, or boards because of your cause. This is actually a sign to you. To be passed along, from one individual or group to another marks that you actually have a cause from God. It also is a sign that your "voice" is confounding the authorities of the day. Continue in your journey, for soon you shall meet the chief authority of the day, you shall meet your Moses!

The Beauty of Names

So often, scripture reveals the naming of children as a significant and important task of the Hebrew people. The names of children are often derived from the prayer life of the parent(s), a strong desire for a child, a vow made unto the Lord, or even the events occurring in the life of the parents at the birth of the child. The names of the children are also considered prophetic, in that what a child is called ultimately drives what the child shall become. Therefore, names are vital to the Hebrew people.

No different is the naming of Zelophehad's daughters. Most often, the naming of children is left to the father, as his voice is the voice of leadership and blessing for the family. What is most interesting among Zelophehad's family is the naming of his daughters. Five in total, one might expect extremely feminine names. However, this is not the case. In fact, it appears that Zelophehad possibly knew he would have daughters and no sons. Of course, this is pure speculation but the reality so noted in scripture is the truth found in the names of his daughters.

It appears that Zelophehad was not dismayed at the birth of five daughters. So many fathers probably would have been gravely disappointed, having no son to carry forth the family name. It is an understood truth amongst the Hebrew people, then and even now that fathers live on through their sons. This is why scripture states such truth as "Jesus, the son of

David, have mercy on me" (Matthew 10:47 KJV). These are the famous words of Blind Bartimeus, who is known as the son of Temaeus. Was Jesus actually David's son? Through the eyes of a Hebrew, the answer is yes because fathers live on through their sons and carry on the family name and blessing.

What happens to the father who has no sons? What is the outcome of the family that has no male heir? What if the father and mother die having only yielded female fruit to live on in their stead? What would happen to the father's estate but more so his name? A lot of questions indeed, but God has revealed a very relative answer to these and more like them. The answer is found in the life of the daughters, those of Zelophehad, who are named for their destiny.

Consider This....

During the times of Jewish Antiquity, the importance of a son was vital. It was considered an absolute necessity to bring forth a son. Households where no son was born were looked upon with dismay or disregard. It was even considered that the father must have sinned in some way that the Lord would not provide him with a son. It was thought to be a judgment from God. Can you imagine what kind of shame Zelophehad felt? He was judged by God to wander in the wilderness until death, as was every person of his generation, but still had no hope for inheritance in the promised-land because he had no son? In essence, he was doubly judged. It would seem that Zelophehad was being punished far more than others of his generation because he simply had no son. If the theological thought of the people is correct, the conclusion of his apparent double judgment would be the utter extinction of his family.

Mahlah

Mahlah, spelled in Hebrew as Machlah, is the eldest of Zelophehad's daughters. Her name means affliction. She is named possibly for the affliction of Egyptian slavery, which was the life of the Hebrew. However, it is more likely that she is named for the period of time where Israel wandered in judgment in the desert. Zelophehad and his wife, descendants of Manasseh, the eldest son of Joseph suffer 40 years with Israel in the desert for their sin of disbelief and utter disobedience. It was in this situation, Mahlah was born.

At first glance, it would appear that her name is a curse unto her. It could be suggested that her presence would be a remembrance of hard, difficult, sinful times. However, she is the eldest of the daughters and came forth and lived in spite of affliction. The affliction did not devour her but fueled her growth and strength. As the eldest, she would have to be able to lead the family, not just in times of prosperity but in times of opposition. Therefore, Mahlah, who is affliction, is not intimidated by affliction but lives through it and rises from it.

From the vantage point of Zelophehad, the affliction is great and most disappointing because it was not supposed to be. His children were to be born in the land of promise, in the land of milk and honey or at worse in en-route. They were to be born in the land of infinite possibilities and his firstborn comes into the earth in a desert place. Zelophehad has escaped the affliction of Pharaoh, now to embrace the affliction of God. It is as if his voice can be heard saying, "Mahlah", I am afflicted.

Noah

Noah, spelled in Hebrew as Noach or No'ah is the second born of Zelophehad and her name has two meanings. The first or the female meaning of the name is to tremble or shake. More than likely, Zelophehad is having mixed emotions. Not prepared for a life in the desert as a nomad, he is now forced to live as one. Israel is not befriended by the inhabitants of Canaan or the surrounding nations and Zelophehad is prob-ably overcome with utter fear. Furthermore, having seen the anger of God burn among Israel in the death of the spies as well as the earth's consumption of Korah and all that rebelled with him, breeds for Zelophehad great fear. Here, we find Zelophehad saying, "I am afraid, trembling, even shaking; Noah".

A very strong argument can be presented based upon trends in scripture. So often, the second child, in particular the second son, inherits the great blessings of the father in lieu of the first born. Such was the case with Ishmael and Isaac, the first two sons of Abraham. Isaac obtained Abra-ham's blessing and Ishmael was exiled. Likewise, a similar circumstance existed with Jacob and Esau. Jacob's character left one wanting initially, but Esau's carnality would have exempted him from blessing and birthright provision regardless of Jacob's character flaws. Furthermore, Jacob's character flaws were rectified and he returned to his birthright and blessing, in the land of Canaan. The greatest example is Adam and the second Adam, Jesus Christ. Adam and Jesus are the only two men begotten directly from God. Adam fell and was condemned. Jesus came that we might have life and life abundantly.

One might ask, why all of the commotion about the blessing? The answer is simple. The blessing of the father is the divine power to prosper regardless of economic conditions. In some instances, the second born even obtains the birthright, or the estate of the father because of the inadequacies often illuminated in the eldest. Therefore, the blessing and birthright are directly tied to the inheritance left of the father.

Noah, Zelophehad's second born daughter is given a name that has a masculine meaning also. Were they mistaken? Did they pray earnestly for a son and not realize they had a daughter? Were they disillusioned in their recognition of the sex of the child? The answer is resoundingly "no" to all the aforementioned. The truth of the matter is more likely the need for rest!

In the days of Methuselah and his son Lamech, judgment was strong upon the earth because of the fall of Adam. Noah, the son of Lamech, the prophet of the Great Flood is the first born after the death of Adam. The descendents of Adam pray that his birth, following Adam's death would bring them rest from their judgment. His birth represented a new day for the family. Noah's birth represented an earth that would become fertile again and yield nutritious, bountiful crops.

As it was with the prophet of the Great Flood, so it is with Zelophehad's second born. Genderism takes second place to the need for relief and rest. Wandering around the same mountain, Sinai for forty years awaiting your death is a most grievous, arduous judgment. Forty years of remembering the greatest mistake of your life. Forty years to reflect on the fact that you did not trust the God, who devoured your enemy, even your oppressor before your very own eyes. Forty years in a dry, arid place, unable to yield any true nourishing crop. What a harsh judgment! It is as if one could hear Zelophehad say in the midst of this trying time, "Noah", interpreted: give me rest.

It was Zelophehad's hope that his Noah's birth would possibly bring some relief or mercy from God to the children of Israel. Possibly, God would repent of His judgment and allow them to enter into the land of promise. It is here the reality unfolds that rest is more than a good night's sleep. Amongst the Hebrew people, rest is being in a place of great provision, peace, and predictability. Predictability as it relates to being settled and established. Zelophehad yearned for Noah!

Hoglah

The third born is Hoglah, whose name means to hop or hobble. This is an interesting name for the third child. Still wandering in the wilderness, destined for death, with the full understanding that this is the judgment of God for your entire generation, Zelophehad, still having obtained no rest now feels that he is hopping or hobbling along.

Wandering can be an awful place in life. It is movement without purpose. It is walking with no definite destination. Wandering is also fatiguing because its end is unknown and may never be known. Zelophehad accompanied by the remaining millions of Israeli's wander in the desert with no definite destination on earth. Their judgment or punishment is to live aimless, fatiguing lives in a place not conducive for productivity. What a judgment! Living in such a way, causes one to stumble, trip, hop, or hobble. The very thing made for your personal transportation, your feet, become unbearable weights about your ankles. Walking gives way to shuffling. Shuffling gives way to dragging. Dragging gives way to hobbling or stumbling, even falling.

When one wanders in desert places, even in the deserts of our lives, feelings of incapacity begin to emerge. One feels like the strength and the assurance of his/her steps is beginning to wane. Doubt and insecurity replace faith and confidence. Midway through judgment or trying times, Zelophehad begins to feel that this will assuredly be the death of him. It is as if we can hear Zelophehad say, "Hoglah" or I am falling.

Milcah

It is suggested, when struggles persist one of two things occur. Long struggles can create depression that continues for many years. Some never recover from it because they allow their depression to devour any thoughts of hope. Hope is a key ingredient that triggers faith to grow and rise regardless of arduous situations.

Conversely, struggles that persist for many years can also cause one to see another vantage point. Long struggles can also birth frustration. Not the type of frustration that causes one to lash out at those surrounding them, but frustration that causes one to behave contrary to their circumstance. It is this frustration that Zelophehad felt and began to behave contrary to his situation. Heretofore, Zelophehad has named his children out of the depravity of his circumstance in the desert. However, now, still in the desert, still subject to the judgment of God, he changes his mind. He turns his efforts and his energy to his posterity. No longer is he hopeful for himself, but Zelophehad embraces what all fathers should embrace; the security and prosperity of his children.

Zelophehad decides, no more affliction and no more yearning for rest where I can find none. No longer will Zelophehad accept stumbling and hobbling along just to make his way in life. He stands up in his soul and his body obeys. His spirit is awakened and Zelophehad chooses royalty, blessing, and promise. He names his fourth born, "Milcah" which means divine or queen. Zelophehad changes the tide of the family and directs them toward their destiny, which is not his destiny. His destiny is judgment ending in death but his heirs are destined for abundant life in the Divine. Zelophehad says, "Milcah". His daughters shall be queens in the Lord's land.

Tirzah

The last of the five daughters is named Tirzah, which means willing or pleasing. Once a person has made the transition from incapable to capable, hopeless to hopeful, doubt to belief, another vantage point is taken. Now preparing his children for greatness, Zelophehad's attention is turned to God. He recognizes that it is God and God alone that has judged his generation. He accepts what God has done and now desires to rear children who are pleasing to the Lord. He desires to present unto God, a family that will put Him first and not their own desires. Zelophehad grasps the purpose of his judgment. Yes, there is a purpose for judgment beyond reprimanding misfit behavior. The judgment was to cleanse Israel of her unfaithfulness and rebellion.

The Israelis' once said, "wherefore hath the Lord brought us unto this land, to fall by the sword, that our wives and our children should be prey? Were it not better for us to return into Egypt?" (Num. 14:3 KJV) It was such a statement that landed such a judgment: "But your little ones, which ye said should be a prey, them will I bring in, and they shall know the land which ye have despised. But as for you, your carcasses, they shall fall in this wilderness." (Num. 14:31-32 KJV) The prey would truly pray. They would be the peculiar people, the kingdom of priests which the Lord declared.

Through all of his toil, Zelophehad became cognizant of the purpose of his judgment. Indeed, Zelophehad was cleansed through his judgment. He now positions the family to walk willingly and pleasing unto the Lord their God. Zelophehad says, "Tirzah, we shall please the Lord."

Dear Daughter,

What do you think of that? Zelophehad's five daughters have such meaningful and purposeful names. It seems that they were, well, selected from birth or possibly prior to birth or conception. Check out the growth in their father as he continues to produce, plant, and name his seed. Wow!

However, I wonder if you really get it. Zelophehad had no sons, only daughters. We can surmise then that he endured the hardship of the wilderness and the ridicule of others but through it all he grew. Now the question is, what was the purpose of all of this? The answer is simple. In order for Israel's light to shine even brighter as a nation, a most peculiar move of God is necessary. It is about to occur and it will continue to separate Israel from other nations. It will even shake the fragile, traditional foundation of Israel itself. God is up to something. What peculiar move is God up to in your life? What's the purpose for such a move? Do you know?

The Difference Between a Cause and a Case

"And Moses brought their cause before the Lord." (Numbers 27:5 KJV)

At first, some may view the possibility of a correlation between a cause and a case and claim it is but a play on words. It may even be suggested that the difference is so miniscule that the relevance of discussion is unmerited. However, history bears a different record.

When considering the difference in a cause and a case one must recognize the depth and vast difference between them. For instance, today, should an event occur that lands one in contradiction with the law, a case is ensued. Accusations and evidence begin to manifest as to why one is possibly guilty of a crime. The arguments are presented in courts of law throughout the country, where a verdict or agreement is reached between the two parties, which serves as justice. This is an example of a case. It is singular in its presentation.

It involves one person against another or one group against another.

A <u>cause</u> is much different. A cause expands beyond he/she that presents or represents it. It invokes the authorities of the day to challenge their thought process and common practices. An example of a cause would be the Women's Suffrage Movement. The movement spanned over a 130 year time period, beginning in 1776 with a letter from Abigail Adams to her husband John Adams, while he was in Philadelphia drafting the Declaration of Independence. She asked him to "remember the ladies". Ignored it was, for the Declaration stated that "All men were created equal".

However, the movement was not stopped. Women began to organize themselves noted by organizations such as Lowell Female Labor Relations Union, which demanded a 10-hour work day for women as well as the National American Women's Suffrage Association, and the National Council of Jewish Women. Women Conventions erupted throughout the north and south. The movement grew and in 1851 took the platform that involved the rights of colored (black) women, who were slaves. This group of women was represented by Harriet Tubman and Sojourner Truth and later birthed the National Association of Colored Women. Sojourner Truth, a black freed slave spoke at a Woman's Convention in Akron, Ohio where she delivered her famous speech, "Ain't I a Woman".

The movement was never stopped, but it was halted by two prolific events: the Civil War, and World War I. While these wars waged, it was women who worked in the factories and machinist shops manufacturing goods and weapons. Finally, after much lobbying and protesting, women received liberty in 1920, with the ratification of the 19th Amendment. From the inception of the country, women were discounted and considered to be second class to men. They were bereft of their "voice" evidenced in the illegality of their right to vote, own property, and in some states work. The focus detailed here was plural not singular. **This was a cause!** It was not a case, for it sought to improve the well being of women throughout the country. If the previous mentioned women and countless others had not found their "voice" and collaborated one with another, their future would have never evolved. Change rarely comes without a struggle and the hardest fought struggle is an ideological one.

Dear Daughter,

Do you have a cause worthy of a platform? Do you have a cause worth fighting for? Is the future well-being of the next generation worthy of you taking a stand now? The stand could be national, state-wide, local, or even within the home? What will be your mark in the earth? Are you concerned about the spiritual, social, and political environment of the next generation or are you completely focused on the state of affairs today? Be honest with yourself! If you truly want a "voice", remember, the "voice" accompanies His cause not your agenda.

The Necessity of a Woman's Voice

*"And it came to pass after the plague, that
the Lord spake unto Moses and unto Eleazar
the son of Aaron the priest, saying, Take the
sum of all the congregation of the children
of Israel, from twenty years old and upward,
throughout their fathers' house, all that are
able to go to war." (Numbers 26:1-2 KJV)*

As the events unfold in the book of Numbers, Moses is occu-
pied with conducting a most tedious and extensive census for
war. These numbers can also be used as a means of dividing
the inheritance of the Lord to His people. This is of utmost
importance, for victory in the land of promise is guaranteed
to them. The real focus and concern is who gets what! This
generation of Israelites is not unbelieving in terms of God's
power, will, and desire for them. They have witnessed their
parents die wandering in the desert. They knew the reason

for their judgment and they also knew they were the hope for the future. With this, this generation had a mind to conquer in the Lord's name. They were not without sin, but certainly their minds were focused on inheriting what God had promised them, which represented the end of this wandering judgment they had been subjected to by the disobedience of their parents.

Now, at a time when Moses is preparing to dispense the land by lot to the tribes of Israel, his final task as leader and prophet, Zelophehad's daughters emerge to state their business. They should have been assembled at the Tabernacle as spectators to the dispensing of the land. Why? Women were not permitted by the cultural norms of the day to receive, transfer, or inherit property. This was the privileged task of men. They should have been represented by either a male heir or a husband. However, they now must emerge as women with "a voice", stating **the cause** of God.

It is with this understanding that Zelophehad's daughters emerge. Their emersion is most interesting and insightful. It is not that women were utterly disregarded in Israel or grossly mistreated as they were in other cultures. However, most assuredly, men held the roles of leadership and legal business was certainly theirs to regulate, as prescribed by the Law of the Lord. Furthermore, princes, elders and clan representatives were all male. However, Zelophehad's daughters had an issue that could not wait for a male voice to express. In all actuality, there was no male voice to express it for them. Here is why: "Our father died in the wilderness, and he was not in the company of them that gathered themselves together against the Lord in the company of Korah; but died in his own sin, and **had no sons**."(Num.27:3) In other words, the daughters of Zelophehad would have been represented if there was a male heir but there was none. If these women do not speak out, their father's name will be blotted out of Israel and they will be subject to poverty.

A cause has emerged without a name. A nation may be subject to a national outcry from its female inhabitants, who are without male representation. Should poverty grip the females of Israel who are without male representation? Should the women be forced to wed unworthy men to escape utter depravity, if their father yielded no male heir? Is this just? Would God be pleased or would this circumstance become the futuristic subject of a prophet's outcry against Israel?

God would not forego an opportunity to rectify an asymptomatic disease when an anecdote is available. Of course, its presentation and application truly distinguish Israel from the other nations. Being asymptomatic it is both unknown and unrecognized. However, what a God Israel serves! He will heal diseases within His choice people that are asymptomatic, yet devastating. Within His apothecary, a compound has been made that will heal Israel of this disease of genderism.

Channeling Emotions before Great Men

Unlike women, men are often out of touch with their own feelings. Innumerable reasons could be given to justify or explain this reality however one of the most prevailing would be learned behavior. Typically, in many cultures, especially those of the Eastern Region, men are expected to be strong, resilient, even callus. Maybe not to this extent in Israel, but none the less, men were expected to be strong and not easily shaken. Therefore, feelings inadvertently are taught to be suppressed.

The great men of Zelophehad's day and those that followed his death were no different. They were not in touch with their emotions and therefore were unable to have discourse, especially pertaining to inheritance laws, with any party that had no control over their emotions. Zelophehad's daughters could have approached the leadership of Israel in a state of panic or distress. The conversation could have been gone one of three ways.

One way would have been a conversation of high pitched screaming as they were fully aware that they were destined for poverty. They could have invoked "noise" as a means of communication. The women could have allowed the emotions of anger, resentment, and indignation to rule their hearts. They could have approached the greatest moment of their lives with vehement speech and sassy body language.

Another alternative would have been to say nothing. They could have employed "no voice". Zelophehad's daughters could have remained silent. This would have been an awful representation of their father's hopes and desires for his family. As many do today, they could have taken the position that holds "someone else will do it". They could have allowed fear to silence them and force them into depravity.

However, Zelophehad's daughters have been adequately prepared for this event. Their father was careful to pour into them all they needed to obtain their inheritance. Their names, in birth order, not only reveal Zelophehad's growth, but the prophetic destiny of his lineage. From mockery to monumental, Zelophehad's name shall ring throughout all Israel as the family of reformers. To that end, Zelophehad's daughters possess, in their bosom, the righteous cause of God and the vehicle to ensure its safe delivery, "a voice"! This is the secret anecdote from God's apothecary.

The great thing about Zelophehad's daughters is their ability to control their emotions. Honestly, the women had every right to "lose it". However, by controlling their emotions they "gained it". Simply put the energy and focus of their emotions was channeled into their cause. This circumstance was not by chance. They were chosen for this situation. God's divine purpose was going to come to pass in their lives through this circumstance. God's purpose always extends beyond the individual who carries it, but always reaches many and impacts their lives in significant ways. Zelophehad's daughters were chosen to speak God's cause before God's great men and set a new order. Their cause would open the door for other women like them to speak the cause of God before the great men of God, who often become religious in place of relational.

Channeling their emotions became the critical element of their argument. Although not discussed or even seen, it was what they did not say or do that had perhaps the greatest impact. They presented a very compelling argument to Moses and the Israeli leadership, which was actually the onslaught of the greatest reform ever noted in Israel. This reform, which heaven completely ratified ushered in a new thought process, unknown to any other nation of the day. In Israel, daughters could now inherit as sons!

By channeling their emotions, Zelophehad's daughters gave Moses and the Israeli leadership an opportunity to hear the cause of God. They provided an argument, in the language and tone that made it easy for Moses and the others to both hear and understand the cause of Zelophehad's daughters. Stumped by women, Moses turned to God for direction. There he discovers God is in agreement with this cause, thereby revealing to us that the cause was God's and God's alone.

The Voices of the Foremothers

It is unknown as to which daughter presented the cause or if each spoke at varying times. What is known is they all came together to the Tabernacle of the Congregation and stood before Moses, Eleazar the priest, and the princes and all the congregation of Israel. This was no small, inconspicuous meeting. It was public and brought to it as attendees, the entire leadership of Israel.

Zelophehad's daughters were not going to be intimidated or buffeted by the attendees of this meeting. In all actuality, they needed the attendees to be present in order that all would know what their cause was and how an injustice was in motion. The injustice befell them not because of any wrongdoing of their own but by the grace of God. Sure, Zelophehad's daughters may not have felt or known this truth at that time but certainly one must accept that their cause was most unique, peculiar and required astute and aristocratic attention.

Having gathered their thoughts, emotions, and considered the cost, Zelophehad's daughters stand as the culmination of women of the patriarchal period. By standing and stating, these women embody the voice that God restored in Sarah. As stated earlier, after the Fall, the scriptures do not detail any woman saying or speaking anything of any significance. It is as if they become no more than procreators of mankind with no recognizable speech. Understand, it is not that they were unable to speak or articulate their thoughts but it appears that their articulation is unconsidered. However, the tide changes with Sarai, who was renamed Sarah. She becomes the woman that God uses to bring about his purpose. Sarah speaks and Abraham listens. Sarah articulates and Abraham considers. Sarah stands in stark contrast to all women who walked before her for she by the grace of God obtained a voice.

Following Sarah, four other women in Jewish Antiquity speak and are heard. Sarah is followed by Rebekkah, who prays unto the Lord and He hearkens to her request and gives her an answer concerning her twins. Rebekkah is followed by Leah, who is disregarded by her father and given to Jacob in trickery. Furthermore, Leah, is hated by her sister and definitely not the choice of her husband. Nevertheless, Leah names her fourth son Judah or praise for she turned unto her God and he delivered her soul from anguish.

During the enslavement of the Hebrew people, Jochebed finds her voice. She refuses to follow the ungodly edict of Pharaoh to turn her son over to be killed. Her voice may not have been audible but certainly her actions were louder than any words she could have spoken. Jochebed hides her baby and then develops a plan with her daughter to ensure the child's safety. Ultimately, as a slave, Jochebed is paid to nurse her baby by Thermitius, Pharaoh's daughter who adopts the baby, names him Moses, and rears him as a prince in Egypt. Her son who should have been killed becomes a prince while she is able to care for him and from a near distance watch him grow.

In the vein of her mother Jochebed, Miriam becomes the fifth woman to utilize her voice. As Moses speaks the Word of God to the destruction of Egypt and Pharaoh, Miriam is overcome with gratitude to the Lord their God. She finds her audible voice in praise unto God. She stands and leads the women of Israel in praise unto God. She takes up a timbrel and speaks praises and sings praises unto God before the entire congregation. "Sing ye to the Lord, for he hath triumphed gloriously; the horse and his rider hath he thrown into the sea." (Ex. 15:21)

It is the work of the foremothers, who are as majorettes for justice, equality, and exhorters for the will of God that converge with Zelophehad's daughters at the Tabernacle. The work of Sarah, Rebekkah, Leah, Jochebed, and Miriam occurred over a 720 year period of time. All of this time, space, work, and wisdom hasten pace to meet Zelophehad's daughters at the Tabernacle. Finally, the work and anointing of the foremothers erupts in a national cause, where the voice of the woman is given a national platform. It is here, we see the elevation of the woman in the eye of the public solidifying her as co-executor and now inheritor of the promise of God.

Their Cause Introduced

Mahlah, Hoglah, Noah, Milcah, and Tirzah stand boldly, not brazenly, before Moses, Eleazar the priest, and before the princes and all the congregation of Israel, at the door of the tabernacle and opened their cause. They said, **"Our father died in the wilderness, and he was not in the company of them that gathered themselves together against the Lord in the company of Korah; but died in his own sin, and had no sons."** (Num. 27:3) This introduces their cause in a factual way. They understand to whom they are speaking and are careful to refrain from emotional outburst of any kind. They simply state the facts that are undeniable and non-confrontational. In essence, they lay a ground work that places everyone on the "same page". In this introduction they are sure to make known that the death of their father was not due to Korah's most repulsive rebellion, in that he attempted to lead Israel back to Egypt. Korah's rebellion was one that stated God's provision was worse than Egyptian bondage. They are sure to separate their father's death from God's judgment on Korah and his cohorts. Rather, they state that Zelophehad died in his own sin, which was the sin of all the generation God led out of Egyptian bondage, the sin of unbelief.

This statement is most respectable. It is understandable and the unfortunate reality of all of the descendents of the Exodus Generation. Their parents died in the wilderness over a forty year judgment of wandering. However, their stating of the cause does not end with this statement. They transition their argument by stating **"and had no sons"**. This statement brings about a shift in the conversation. "And had no sons" speaks volumes to a leadership that respects a man and his sons. "And had no sons" drives the conversation from the status of a case to a cause. "And had no sons"!

The Name of the Father

*"Our Father which art in heaven,
hallowed be thy name. Thy kingdom
come, thy will be done in earth, as it is
in heaven." (Matthew 6:9-10 KJV)*

As mentioned earlier, God's kingdom is not like man's kingdom. Israel was to replicate God's heavenly kingdom in the earth. Literally, bring heaven to earth. As such, in Israel, God is concerned about each individual and the hairs that are numbered upon their head. God is focused on every aspect, of every person, of every family, of every clan, of every tribe in Israel. The small things matter to God just as much as the big things. Therefore, His kingdom is established on the complete recognition of every family. This is why Deuteronomy 25:5-10 resound's the importance of every family line being preserved. In short, should a man die who is married, and have a brother, the living brother is to take his deceased brother's wife as his own and raise up seed to his brother's name. He is to take her as his own wife and impregnate her in the stead of his deceased brother, "And it shall be, that the firstborn which she beareth shall succeed in the name of his brother which is dead, **that his name be not put out of Israel.**" (v.6) God's intent for His kingdom is to lose no one and to ensure the legacy of everyone. Truly, the kingdom is to last forever.

However, the daughter's of Zelophehad did not meet the criteria of this law but were subject to extinction of their father's name. Here is why. Zelophehad was the father of five girls, Mahlah, Noah, Hoglah, Milcah, and Tirzah. They were of the tribe of Manasseh, who is the son of Joseph. Zelophehad had no sons therefore, legally he had no heir to carry his name, seeing that daughter's take the name of their husbands and continue that house. Based upon simple genealogical principles, Zelophehad's house would go extinct because he had no male heir. Their question is **"Why should the name of our father be done away from among his family, because he hath no son? Give unto us therefore a possession among the brethren of our father."** (Num. 27:4 KJV) His name was going to be blotted out of Israel, as if he had sinned a great sin and received such a harsh judgment. His sin, was his own, and was not aligned with Korah's rebellion. Therefore, he was not subject to utter destruction and extinction. Although his life did not subject him to such destruction, none the less it was impending!

Therefore, based upon the law alone, the daughter's had no case of inheritance. Their father had no sons for heirs therefore it could be argued that it was the Lord's will for their father's name to be blotted out of Israel. Be mindful, that the law is a taskmaster, in that it exposes sin and provides vindication for it. However, it does not have the power to convert but rather has the power to condemn. The law is not designed to navigate spiritual matters, but rather carnal, objective ones.

The Apostle Paul states this well when he writes to the Romans, "**For the promise, that he should be the heir of the world, was not to Abraham, or to his seed, through the law, but through the righteousness of faith. For if they which are of the law be heirs, faith is made void, and the promise made of none effect: Because the law worketh wrath: for where no law is, there is no transgression.**" (4:13-15 KJV)

In essence, the case of Zelophehad's daughters, which is no case at all, is technically not a legal one but a spiritual one; it is a cause. The law does not address their circumstance because no sin is implicated. The law does not confront their issue because no sin has been committed to bring this circumstance into existence. This situation gives rise to a higher level of governance. It is one fitted for the divine wisdom of God Himself.

The cause of Zelophehad's' daughters stumps Moses, but Moses is a man of integrity and great wisdom. He also knows the extent of his wisdom and takes the matter to the wisest of all, God the Father. A human can only understand a case. He/She alone is not able to decipher a cause. Such must be decoded and revealed by God to man. **"And Moses brought their cause before the Lord."** (Numbers 27:5 KJV) It was at this point, that the voice of the women reached He who had given it. And the voice of God said, **"the daughters of Zelophehad speak right: thou shalt surely give them a possession of an inheritance among their father's brethren; and thou shalt cause the inheritance of their father to pass unto them."**(Num 27:7 KJV)

Faith is the key to inheritance. It is the force that reigns above the law. It is the force that will bring amendments to the law. The cause of Zelophehad's' daughters render this verdict from God: **"And thou shalt speak unto the children of Israel, saying, If a man die, and have no son, then ye shall cause his inheritance to pass unto his daughter."**(Num. 27:8 KJV) The law will always be subject to faith because faith is the key to inheriting the promises of God. The purpose of the law is to expose sin, not to address matters that are not derivatives of sin.

Dear Daughter,

Sometimes your circumstance is not addressed by the letter of the law and your predicament may fall short of the expressed law and cause them that rule or judge to ponder. Even more, you may be subject to impending danger although you have done nothing to justify such. It is in these times, that you must rise above that which is written and speak that which is spiritual and just. If the rule of the earth is unjust, rise to heaven for as it is in heaven so shall it be in the earth. Invoke your "voice".

SECTION IV:
MAINTAINING YOUR VOICE
THROUGH LIFE AND ON...

An Equitable Agreement

"A false balance is abomination to the Lord: but a just weight is his delight." (Proverbs 11:1 KJV)

The victory God granted the daughters of Zelophehad changed the course of Israeli history. Literally, God defeated the custom that supported genderism. It was forever renounced when He spoke to Moses, "The daughters of Zelophehad speak right: thou shalt surely give them a possession of an inheritance among their father's brethren;" (Num. 27:7). This was great news for Mahlah, Noah, Hoglah, Milcah, and Tirzah. However, with inheritance comes responsibility.

Sons inherit the father's land and in so doing they take on a great responsibility. Inheriting the father's land implies that one will reside on the land, cultivate it, and continue the father's work, even in a greater way. Sons do not move off of the land for it is their blessing from both their earthly father and their heavenly father. The land provides a place for them to do what they were created to do, which is to be fruitful, multiply, replenish the earth, and execute dominion. God made a place for Israel, in particular Israel's sons to perform their natural work.

Sons also marry daughters in Israel and have children. The name of their father continues and the father's then live through the sons. In essence, a son's father may die, but his name and his work will forever be remembered because of the land and the son's ability to continue the work of the father. Also, the father is remembered by the inheritance he leaves for his children's children. Literally, his grandchildren benefit from the wealth he accumulates and the cycle continues. Father's live through the sons perpetually.

With the recent amendment God has made to the Law of Moses as well as the acceptable custom in Israel, new implications arise that can compromise the integrity of the Law of Moses. If Zelophehad's daughters are to inherit the land that would be their father's, the tribe of Manasseh could be in danger of a reduction in their lot. Specifically, Zelophehad's daughters are truly that, daughters. This means they can become the wife of any man in Israel. They could marry men from the tribes of Judah, Benjamin, Simeon, Naphtali, Ephraim, Dan or any other.

With this in mind, should they marry a man from another tribe the inheritance that was given to the entire tribe of

Manasseh would be compromised. Manasseh is in danger of losing a portion of their lot to another tribe due to the fact that Zelophehad's daughters were standing in the stead of a son. Their potential marriage endangers the entire tribe and the same could become a reality in other tribes as well. There has to be some additional legislative work to ensure that God's amendment does not undermine the inheritance of others.

Again, Moses consults the Lord, who gave him the law and returns to them saying, "The tribe of the sons of Joseph hath said well. This is the thing which the Lord hath commanded concerning the daughters of Zelophehad, saying, Let them marry to whom they think best; only to the family of the tribe of their father shall they marry." (Num. 36:5-6) This amendment also includes any of the daughters of Israel, who become inheritors. In other words, the reform brought on by Zelophehad's daughters cover every daughter of Israel. What a great work Zelophehad's daughters have wrought and even more is their willingness to do what is best for everyone impacted. Zelophehad's daughters are not selfish women, but women of God who are as their foremother's were; always working for the benefit of the nation of Israel.

Living in the Blessing

*"The thief cometh not, but for to steal, and
to kill, and to destroy: I am come that ye
might have life, and that they might have
it more abundantly." (John 10:10 KJV)*

"Even as the Lord commanded Moses, so did the daughters
of Zelophehad: For Mahlah, Tirzah, and Hoglah, and Milcah,
and Noah, the daughters of Zelophehad, were married unto
their father's brothers' sons: And they were married into the
families of the sons of Manasseh the son of Joseph, and their
inheritance remained in the tribe of the family of their father."
(Num. 36:10-12). The responsibility was no less for Zelophehad's daughters as it would have been if they were male heirs.
They remain on the land, marry within the tribe, and carry
forth the work and name of their father in Israel. He will not
be forgotten or blotted out, but Zelophehad shall live on as a
father in Israel.

Likewise, Mahlah, Tirzah, Hoglah, Milcah, and Noah live on carrying their father's name. They wed men from within the tribe and the first born carries forth the name of Zelophehad. Rest has come for Zelophehad's family. They could have been destined for sickness, poverty and disease, but because they utilized the voice God gave them, in a Godly manner, they reap a great harvest. The wonderful thing is their purpose for invoking the voice God gave them was in honor of their father.

The hearts of Zelophehad's daughters were upright in the sight of God. Therefore, God hearkened unto them as he had other women who's hearts were tender toward Him and His cause. The truth of the matter is Zelophehad's daughters brought the cause of God before God's men. God's men consulted Him and He confirmed His own cause. When a woman has a heart after God, His cause becomes her cause. When she speaks His cause, she speaks His Word, and to that end she will never be ashamed.

Now, in Israel, the daughters have obtained a liberty that could have only come from God. Daughters have now been escalated and elevated in society. Fathers no longer have to stress or feel ashamed because they have no sons. Now, daughters can inherit as sons!

Passing on the Voice

"This day shall be for you a memorial day, and you shall keep it as a feast to the Lord; throughout your generations, as a statute forever, you shall kept it as a feast." (Exodus 12:14 KJV)

One of the most difficult tasks of any matriarch or patriarch is the passage of family heirlooms, money, and property. These are the very things that cause such an upheaval after the death of a matriarch or patriarch. One brother desires the car that was left to another brother or one sister desires the family china that was left to another sister. The list can be endless and the bickering ridiculous. What a shame it is to find that children no longer argue or strive after the blessing of the matriarch or patriarch.

During the times of the patriarchs of Israel, brothers would literally fight for the spoken spiritual blessing of the father. Culturally, it was accepted that such was to be given to the eldest son but so often in the lineage of Christ we find the second son becoming the benefactor of the blessing.

So then, the question arises, what is meant by the blessing? In order to bring into perspective the true meaning of the blessing, an understanding of both birthright and blessing must be provided. First, the birthright shall be explained. The birthright, in short is what is basically listed above as the items of tangibility of which the modern-day family bicker. During the times of Jewish Antiquity and later in the Conquering Years as well as the Monarchy Years, the birthright was the land of the father. This is a physical inheritance. It included the servants associated with the father's land, possibly a house or houses, vineyards, ranches, and the responsibility of family leadership.

Beyond the birthright is the blessing. The blessing was a spiritual inheritance. It was often passed on by the "laying on of hands" from the father to his son. The blessing was the "God ordained power to accumulate wealth and maintain favor in all dealings. The blessing is more than just wealth accumulation however, it is also the ability to hear the voice of God and experience intimate encounters with Him." (Ray, 2009). The blessing was the very thing that made Jacob great. Jacob was able to thrive wherever he was because the blessing of Abraham was upon him. He could sojourn in a foreign land and still be blessed above all inhabitants of that land.

Another unfortunate reality of today is many patriarchs and matriarchs feel as if there is no blessing to pass on to their children for nothing was passed to them. So it is, now, they die silently leaving their children and grandchildren as well in a vacuum. It is supposed to be that the patriarch and/or matriarch leave a spiritual word to their children and pass on the work of the Lord to at least one of them. However, if the patriarch or the matriarch has no work from the Lord, what then can be passed on? This vacuum is the work of the enemy, for if no work from the Lord is passed on, the enemy of our souls has the opportunity to insert a curse where a blessing should have been. Thus, we have generations now of people who do not know the Lord. This results in the apostasy of a nation.

This then sheds light on the state of many women and girls today. Nothing of spiritual significance has been passed on to them so they become lawless and "noisy". Their behavior is unbalanced, and many are aggressive in the place of assertiveness. Their words are as venom when they should be a salve. Some become the objects of abuse and veer to another spectrum of self-centeredness, "no voice". Because of fear, oppression, and cultural norms, her voice has been muted. The greater good of all is forsaken due to fear and is replaced by the preservation of the best interest of the individual. Such is the sad reality when curses are passed in the place of a blessing. Generations of "noisy" or "voiceless" women are cultivated. This is the work of the enemy.

So then, what can be done to alter this treacherous pattern? Christ explains it best in his further response to Nicodemus, a ruler of the Jews of the Pharisees when he says, "Verily, verily, I say unto thee, except a man be born of water and of the Spirit, he cannot enter into the kingdom of God. That which is born of the flesh is flesh; and that which is born of the Spirit is spirit." (John 3:5-6). If this treacherous pattern is to stop, women must:

1.   Repent unto God of their sins. This means to accept Jesus Christ as Lord and Savior, submit to His authority and renounce all agendas. Many have accepted him as Savior but not as Lord. This speaks to his position as ruler. His rule is quite different from that of man however. He is kind, understanding, loving unconditionally, and gentle. He is not an abuser, a user, or a deceiver. He leads you to green pastures and restores your soul. Submission to his authority will ensure your safety, well being, and prosperity in His kingdom. It is also important to renounce your agendas because Christ will not compete with alternative plans. He is the Lord of lords and King of kings and beside him there is none other. Therefore, put away your ideas and concepts of the flesh and learn of the Spirit so that you

can reap a spiritual harvest that will sustain you and others.

2. Worship God in Spirit and in truth. True worshippers are not just found in corporate worship service. True worshippers worship God at home, in their cars, on their jobs, and even on lunch breaks. They are people who are often alone, peaceful, and comfortable. Sure they would have many friends and acquaintances but idle conversation, gossip, and silly chattering is repulsive to them because it subtracts from their spiritual bank and this is a transaction which they cannot afford. Therefore, they smile, are kind, and leave sufficient space between themselves and others who are not true worshippers.

3. Receive His plan. People who truly worship God lose their agendas and receive His plan. His plan brings them fulfillment, peace, hope, encouragement, and most of all focus. Their gifts become evident to them, which are directly tied to His plan and purpose for their life. Things begin to make sense. Their spiritual gifts as well as their earthly talents begin to align with God's plan and purpose. To this end, the true worshippers become immersed in God and completely focused on their life's purpose, which is to fulfill His

will. Their role is obvious to them and great joy engulfs their soul. It is unspeakable!

When repentance, worship, and receiving have occurred women will find themselves as Zelophehad's daughters did. Doors will begin to open that have historically been closed. Leaders will be confounded by the knowledge, wisdom, and the request of women. Furthermore, women will find themselves before great men, who will in turn be forced to turn to the High Holy Court of God for an answer to their request. All of these things are evident when a true "voice" is invoked. The curse of "noise" and "no voice" will be broken, genderism will be defeated, and inheritance will be a reality. Now, you are in the position to pass on a spiritual inheritance of "a voice".

In closing, the success of Zelophehad's daughters was not political but spiritual. Their words were not their own but God's. They were not inflicted with a case but endowed with a cause. Their life's purpose, was not to obtain an inheritance for themselves only but to ensure that all women could inherit in Israel, the kingdom of God on earth. To that end, their cause came accompanied with a "voice" to both articulate it and embody it. Indeed, it had been passed on from the matriarch's of old. It was that "voice" which brought forth Isaac, blessed Jacob, comforted Leah, encouraged Jochebed, and permitted Miriam to praise God in freedom. So now, the question becomes, do you have a "voice"?

One Final Note

Dear Daughter,

This final note is written to you to relay one final command. Yes, a command! This is the command God gave the soon to be liberated Israelites as they were preparing to hastily depart Egypt. The entire focus of the Passover was to be the beginning of months for Israel and stand as a memorial.

Why a memorial? A memorial is remembrance of a pivotal event or person that had such an impact on the lives of many that it is marked. The mark, which is a day or some set time period, serves as an opportunity to recall the individual or the event that has had such a remarkable impact on people throughout the region. This memorial is something that all can share in and reflect. For instance, Memorial Day in the United States serves as a day to remember all of the fallen soldiers of wars past. We honor and regard their sacrifice, which has made life as we know it possible, even unto this day.

Likewise, today, you should mark as a memorial. This is a day of significance and pivotal change in your life. As it was for Israel, so it is for you. Israel was oppressed and enslaved due to their numbers and their race. Yes another "ism", racism. For over 400 years, this was the life of an Israelite. However, on that day, when the Lord commanded the Passover, Israel was forever changed. They were delivered from oppression and from the state of "no voice" to freedom, liberty, and a "voice".

So it is with you, you are released from having "no voice" or from one creating "noise". You are delivered from the oppression of "genderism" and released to the state God has designed for you and millions of others. That is, to not just speak, for such is the simple application of the faculties of your body. You are rather, released to pursue God, His righteous cause, and utilize the "voice" that He grants for the announcement, effectuation, and fulfillment of His Will!

May God Bless and Enrich You!

Another Son,

Tommy

"For as many as are led by the Spirit of God, they are the sons of God. For ye have not received the spirit of bondage again to fear; but ye have received the Spirit of adoption, whereby we cry, Abba, Father."
(Romans 8:14-15 KJV)

Endnotes

1. www.headcoverings-by-devorah.com/NamesWomen-Torah.htm
2. www.headcoverings-by-devorah.com/NamesMenTorah.htm
3. www.jewfaq.org/torah.htm
4. Professor Barry J. Beitzel et al. Biblica: The Bible Atlas. Global Book Publishing, 2006.
5. William Whiston, A.M., Translator. The Works of Josephus: New Updated Edition. Hendrickson Publishers, Inc., 1987.
6. Thomas Ray, III. Concepts for Sound, Biblical Teaching and Extrapolation. Self Published, 2009.
7. Donald C. Stamps, Chief Editor, J. Wesley Adams, Associate Editor. The Full Life Study Bible. Zondervan Publishing House, 1992.
8. Life Application Study Bible, New International Version. Tyndale House Publishers, Inc and Zondervan Publishing House, 1991.

.

www.ingramcontent.com/pod-product-compliance
Lightning Source LLC
Chambersburg PA
CBHW020509100426
42813CB00030B/3172/J